WINDING PATHS

PHOTOGRAPHS BY BRUCE CHATWIN

Introduction by
Roberto Calasso

JONATHAN CAPE
LONDON

Published by Jonathan Cape 1999

2 4 6 8 10 9 7 5 3 1

Text and photographs © 1998 The Legal and Personal Representatives of Bruce Chatwin

Design © 1998 Adelphi Edizioni S.P.A. Milan

First published in Great Britain in 1999 by
Jonathan Cape
Random House, 20 Vauxhall Bridge Road,
London SW1V 2SA

Random House Australia (Pty) Limited
20 Alfred Street, Milsons Point, Sydney,
New South Wales 2061, Australia

Random House New Zealand Limited
18 Poland Road, Glenfield,
Auckland 10, New Zealand

Random House South Africa (Pty) Limited
Endulini, 5A Jubilee Road, Parktown 2193, South Africa

Random House UK Limited Reg. No. 954009
A CIP catalogue record for this book is available from the British Library

ISBN 0 224 06050 3

Papers used by Random House UK Limited are natural,
recyclable products made from wood grown in sustainable forests.
The manufacturing processes conform to the environmental
regulations of the country of origin

Typeset by MATS, Southend-on-Sea, Essex
Printed and bound in Italy

Contents

CHETTE-WYNDE

BY ROBERTO CALASSO

This publication could never have happened without the co-operation of Elizabeth Chatwin, who has generously put the materials in her possession and, even more importantly, the precious archives of her memory at my disposal. Chatwin, in fact, never bothered to organize the photographs he took, and it was sometimes hard to identify places. We therefore owe all the captions to Elizabeth Chatwin herself.

A word of thanks must also go to Nicholas Shakespeare, to whom we owe the Chronology, and to Maddalena Buri, who oversaw the production of the book with such tenacity and dedication.

R.C.

I never saw Chatwin with a camera. I was unaware that a camera was ever stowed in his meagre baggage – though I could easily have told you with complete certainty which tie (stars on a blue background) he had with him. I had only seen the stunning photographs that illustrate *In Patagonia*. And I had heard of Rebecca West's famous *bon mot* when she saw them: 'They are so beautiful that not one word of the text was necessary.' As with many *bons mots*, this one was obviously untrue. As with many *bons mots*, it contained a deeper truth. For there is something about the short, numbered chapters of *In Patagonia* that suggests an analogous series of photographs. One can imagine those numbers on the margins of a film slowly unrolling before our eyes. No matter if those fragments frequently deal with insubstantial, fantastic stories; their inner character is always visual, tactile, as if they were inviting us, phrase by phrase, to pass our eyes or fingertips over a surface that has something to tell us before and beyond all meaning. (A sense for surfaces: I believe this was a kind of spirit guide for Chatwin, in his prose, his photographs, his taste for certain objects).

So we never talked about photography. And yet there was very little we did not talk about. We never knew where our conversations would lead. A pleasure that must be congenial to nomads. Even the words themselves wandered along 'winding paths' (for which the Anglo-Saxon equivalent, *chette-wynde*, gave rise to the name Chatwin, at least according to his Uncle Robin – or was it his Aunt Ruth who mentioned it?), and the resulting journey was punctuated by explosions: a story usually, or some detail, an anecdote, a word, a colour, the smoke provided by his bursts of laughter, oscillating between the childish and the mechanical, as if produced by rotating cog-wheels. But a conversation described is always slightly frustrating for those who would have liked (or would still like) to take part. By a stroke of luck, and by a strange chance, I can quote an example of such a conversation, complete in itself and sketched by Chatwin's own pen. One day, in Milan, he wrote in a tattered visitor's book ('Liste des Visites, or a Carriage Companion, Printed for William Marsh, 137 Oxford Street') the following lines:

Une Historie de la Bourgeoisie Française

In a restaurant we sat next to two hatchet-faced women who argued mercilessy as to whether an Alaska was the same as *une île flottante* or *une omelette norvé*gienne. One of the husbands was fat, piglike, and wore six gold rings; the other was a reincarnation of Monsieur Homais. He was, it turned out, also a pharmacist. He observed that there was one dish he would never tire of: *un gigot d'agneau, pommes dauphinoise*. Over coffee he said the following: 'Je vais vous raconter l'histoire d'un homme qui est parti pour son voyage de noces avec sa nouvelle femme et, pendant le voyage, elle était tuée, meurtrie par quelqu'un. Et lui, pour oublier ses tristes souvenirs, est parti pour . . .' and at this point one expected the words 'Tahiti' or 'la Nouvelle Calédonie' . . . but no! 'il est parti pour la Belgique où il est devenu président d'une société de fabrication du chocolat . . . de la laiterie . . . et même les produits chimiques'.

Bruce Chatwin, 20 October, '87

This enchanting cameo preserves Chatwin's tone of voice perfectly – and demonstrates how he used to capture a scene (or a snapshot) by clipping it out with his prehensile ear (or eye) from the hubbub of a restaurant (or the desert), isolating it, paring it down, impressing it upon the page with a dryness and rapidity of touch. More than sensitivity, this was simply his make-up, how his mind worked. It explains why innumerable, diligent English-speaking travel writers of today and yesterday manage to provoke only respectful yawns despite all their pedantic and dogged conscientiousness, while those episodes from *In Patagonia*, carved upon the void, are still vibrantly alive. Of course there are exceptions, and Chatwin was well aware of them: the neurotic Robert Byron, the mischievous Evelyn Waugh, and the dry Wilfred Thesiger . . . But I can understand why he hated to be called a travel-writer. . .

To pass on to another subject (and I believe we talked about this), I have long suspected that for the English the idea of travel has always had a higher potentiality for eroticism and horror than it does for other Europeans. The English Channel is more than a stretch of frequently rough water, it is a metaphysical barrier. 'Immorality begins on the dock at Calais' was the admonishment pronounced by a haughty spinster while taking tea with Ermyntrude, aunt of the eighteen-year-old Evangeline who, fresh from her finishing school, could not wait to 'experiment' on the Continent. (Where are we? Of course in Cole Porter's *Nymph Errant* . . .)

Why should this be? Perhaps because no other European country has ever developed to the same degree the idea of coinciding with the natural order of things. The rhythm of afternoon tea and evening tipple is not fundamentally distinguishable from that of the first appearance of cuckoos in the spring, celebrated by letters to the *Times*. There is a sense of cosmic order in domestic routine that makes the word *outlandish* appear, by contrast, not only vaguely menacing but of more remote and more sinful implication than its equivalent in any other language.

Yet it was this *outlandishness* (which is not only geographical: there is nothing more *outlandish* than some reading matter, or certain ways or reading) in which Chatwin was immersed all his life, by constitution, by vocation, by fate. This was perhaps the quality that (besides his own good looks) helps to explain both the suspicion with which his writing was greeted in his lifetime and his rapid rise to cult status, even though tempered by some residual rancour which continues to surface – never more clearly than in an article lambasting him for his notebooks *en moleskine* bought, to make matters worse, in Paris! And the writer added: Could he not have bought them from his local stationer? This is a case of the cultural police in action, sniffing out the aesthete, to say nothing of the snob, lurking behind the *outlandishness*. Nowadays, when massacres are two-a-penny, this is the moral criticism most frequently heard. The charge of aestheticism is levelled first and foremost at those who know how to *see*. Chatwin, with his all-penetrating eye, stood out even among the usual suspects. (I now wonder whether his malevolent article about – strangely enough – Robert Louis Stevenson, also guilty of being incurably *outlandish*, was not a perverse response to all this, as if Chatwin were showing his enemies the most effective way of landing their blows upon himself.)

Let's talk a bit about nomads now, since we often used to speak about them. (For Chatwin a talk about nomads was like a medieval theologian discussing the Trinity.) Thinking about it, it would seem that in recent years, and this was more evident in the mid seventies, nomads have come to be regarded as the Good Guys. Nomadic life suggests freedom from oppressive rule, an escape from the persecution of the New Man, who after all is at best a gaoler, more frequently a spy. In July 1972 I was at Cérisy-la-Salle for the Nietzsche Conference. Deleuze (whose *Anti-Oedipe* had just been published) gave a paper on what he called *Pensée nomade*. There was already a slight odour of canonisation ('We all know the nomads are unhappy under our régime: we obstruct them at all turns, it is difficult for them to survive. And Nietzsche lived like one of those nomads reduced to a shadow of their former selves, moving as he did from furnished room to furnished room').

I must have been sceptical even then, because I responded to Deleuze (and to the overeager university students pressing him on all sides) with some words on the theme of parody: 'I would like to return to the question posed at the end of Deleuze's paper, asking who are the nomads of today. . . We have heard about Pop Art, spontaneous groups, aleatory music, kidnappings and happenings. We even got as far as evoking, in an unwittingly revealing way, a so-called "popular psychiatry" based upon the writings of Nietzsche. I can accept that all these things have an undoubted connection with Nietzsche, but only in the sense that they are symptomatic of a world that is becoming increasingly a colossal parody of Nietzsche's ideas.'

It is with some unease that I note how much these words are coloured by the spirit of those times and by the memory (almost idyllic compared to the grim opacity of today) of those discussions. But that same Zeitgeist also affected the great project that Chatwin carried around like a basket on his back that might well have been defined not as *The Nomadic Alternative* (a good enough title although it, too, smacks of the spirit of those years) but more widely and ambitiously as *A History of the World Seen Through Nomad Eyes*. There is another point to be made here. For a 'scholar-gypsy' such as Chatwin (the brilliant definition is Salman Rushdie's, 'scholar-gypsy' implying in this case a scholar that other scholars cannot take seriously – a 'gypsy', in fact – but one who reads, sniffs around and identifies the texts essential to a particular discipline years, sometimes decades, before the scholars who will then ponder wisely over those same texts) – to resume: for a 'scholar-gypsy' nomads are a foretaste of heaven itself. How many names of peoples, rivers, ruins to conjure with. Inaccessible, ominous, refractory! Erotic material for every *delectatio morosa*. . . What tales of subterfuge, intrigue, conquest and desolation emerge from the writings of the great scholars of central Asia. . . This is the ultimate exoticism: to read Markwart! To read Pelliot! To read Barthold! . . . Perhaps while leafing through the intoxicating pages of these philologists, Chatwin came across the word that, thinking about it now, describes him most accurately: *qalandar*. W. Ivanow once confessed that he spent forty years trying to define the term. To no avail. And the most that Henry Corbin would do was explain that in Persian poetry, the word, of pre-Islamic origin, was synonymous with 'religious migrant, as free as the wind'. Someone else defined these people as 'wandering Dervishes, tellers of intricate tales, sons of kings often born in small apartments, sometimes crippled by fate'. Very little is known about them for sure. But the sources always insist on two points: the real *qalandars* belong to no recognised religious cult and never sleep in the same place two nights running. The 'book about the nomads', of which we talked throughout the time we knew each other, was to have included all this and much else besides. The problem of the form it should take vexed him constantly. I have before me a letter written by Chatwin from Jodhpur in February 1986: 'I've had a terrible time with the "Australian" book: have torn up 3 successive drafts: only to find, borrowing a leaf from *La Rovina di Kasch*, that the only way is the "cut-up" method.'

Once he told me that he was thinking of casting it in the form of a long letter, of which I was to be the recipient, called *Letter from Middle Bore*. Then I learnt from Salman Rushdie that he was thinking of a dialogue between two men sitting under a tree in Alice Springs. Rushdie felt that he was the stand-in for one of the men. He was going to call the book *Arkady*. None of this came about. In the end the form of the book was determined overwhelmingly by the onset of his illness and the frantic need to get it done while he could. So the story duly opened on the rugged, wild landscape of the notebooks *en moleskine*, whose number could have increased many times over without ever yielding to that deplorable '*rage de conclure*' (Flaubert).

I ask myself now what it was that held everything together, the books, the photographs, the essential gesture of his character. I would say that above all it was the cut, the essential gift, one imagines, of the diamond cutters of Amsterdam, the ability to find the angle that will release the light within. And also a certain serendipity of vision. And then that element lying at the heart of all theological writings: Grace. Perhaps nothing more, certainly nothing less. It was this that gave Chatwin that 'unerring sense of composition' we find as much in his photographs as it is in the paragraphs of *Utz*. Yeats once wrote: 'I have often had the fancy that there is some one myth for every man, which if we but knew it, would make us understand all he did and thought.' Not, perhaps, entirely true, but still a very beautiful and thought-provoking sentence. If I pull together all I saw and thought of Chatwin, I find that one word constantly recurs: *journey*. And with the word come two images that circumscribe it, since these days the word 'journey' has come to encompass almost everything. What was the first journey, or at least the model for us of every journey? Certainly not that of Odysseus, which was a homecoming. A homecoming can never have the essentially freewheeling quality of real travel, which is a total surrender to the unknown. We must go back further in time, to around a thousand years before Homer. Here we find a text carved on tablets of clay found among the ruins of Nippur: *The Descent of Inanna*. This is how it opens (in the translation of S.N. Kramer):

From the Great Above she opened
    her ear to the Great Below
From the Great Above the goddess
    opened her ear to the Great Below
From the Great Above Inanna
    opened her ear to the Great Below.

Repetition with progressive identification of the subject is a rhetorical device peculiar to Sumerian texts. At the beginning the subject is a simple pronoun, 'she'. Then we discover the 'she' is a 'goddess'. Then that the 'goddess' is Inanna, the radiant, the sacred prostitute, whose carriage is drawn by lions. The moment that Inanna, from the skies (for Inanna is also the planet Venus) 'opens her ear' to the Great Below, which is the infernal region, the dark kingdom from which there is no return, ruled over by her sister Ereshkigal, is the moment that travel is born. She was the first to feel that restlessness, that *horreur du domicile*, even if her 'domicile' was the whole expanse of heaven and earth. She was the first Arctic Tern, that 'beautiful white bird, that flies from the North Pole to the South Pole and back again'. Life was overflowing in her, so that she could not rest until she had had the seven locks of the realm of death opened for her and ended up becoming a prisoner there. That's how mad the undertaking was, how fraught with peril even for a goddess (her shining body was eventually found hanging on a nail in the underworld like a carcass in a butcher's shop.) And at the end, we still haven't answered the question, what reason would a god have for travelling? Conquest, sometimes, a *translatio imperii*, as for Apollo at Delphi, where he descended like a hawk from Olympus, looking for a 'source of sweet water'. But not even a god can conquer the underworld. So what was Inanna seeking? Perhaps all she wanted was to *see* something. To open one's eyes and look is the primordial, irreducible prerequisite of knowledge. It is also the origin of every photograph. Perhaps, as Brodsky wrote in his *Letter to Horace*, it is true that 'reality, like the Pax Romana, wants to expand'. This is why Inanna, sovereign of all, was seeking a Beyond made of shadows and dust. This is the inaugural journey that precedes and informs every other journey. As a traveller, I believe that Chatwin was a devotee of Inanna rather than one among the myriad descendants of Odysseus. But there is another image, closer to us and consonant, I believe, with Chatwin's understanding of the myth of travel. It comes from Chateaubriand, a writer we never talked about, whom Chatwin may not have liked and whose style was certainly in direct contrast to his own. Enemies of Chateaubriand have frequently abused his *Itinéraire de Paris à Jérusalem*, adducing a whole variety of criticisms, calling it unreliable, a collage of the works of others, the diary of someone who tired of everything in no time and was motivated only by a mania to be on the move. At first Chateaubriand defended himself along typically pompous lines (going on a pilgrimage, doing it for love, etc.), but in one of his rare moments of sharp candour he said: 'I was looking for *images*, nothing else.' Here speaks the writer, all writers. And in Chatwin's case the writer was one of those rare and daring souls who knew how to follow Noel Coward's esoteric maxim: 'Never let anything artistic stand in your way.' Even when he became – on occasion – a memorable photographer.

Roberto Calasso

WINDING PATHS

PHOTOGRAPHS BY BRUCE CHATWIN

Winding Paths

The etymology of 'Chatwin' is obscure, but my bassoon-playing Uncle Robin maintained that 'chette-wynde' meant 'winding path' in Anglo-Saxon.

Children need paths to explore, to take bearings on the earth in which they live, as a navigator takes bearings on familiar landmarks. If we excavate the memories of childhood, we remember the paths first, things and people second – paths down the garden, the way to school, the way round the house, corridors through the bracken or long grass. Tracking the paths of animals was the first and most important element in the education of early man.

Bruce Chatwin

I remember the fantastic homelessness of my first five years. My father was in the Navy, at sea. My mother and I would shuttle back and forth, on the railways of wartime England, on visits to family and friends.

All the frenzied agitation of the times communicated itself to me; the hiss of steam on a fogbound station; the double clu-unk of carriage doors closing; the drone of aircraft, the searchlights, the sirens; the sound of a mouth-organ along a platform of sleeping soldiers.

Home, if we had one, was a solid black suitcase called the Rev-Robe, in which there was a corner for my clothes and my Mickey Mouse gas-mask. I knew that, once the bombs began to fall, I could curl up inside the Rev-Robe, and be safe.

At boarding school I was an addict of atlases and was always being ostracised for telling tall stories.

Bruce Chatwin's apartment at Albany, London, 1981

Instead, we should perhaps allow human nature an appetitive drive for movement in the widest sense. The act of journeying contributes towards a sense of physical and mental well-being, while the monotony of prolonged settlement or regular work weaves patterns in the brain that engender fatigue and a sense of personal inadequacy. Much of what the ethologists have designated 'aggression' is simply an angered response to the frustrations of confinement...

The tenacity with which nomads cling to their way of life, as well as their quick-witted alertness, reflects the satisfaction to be found in perpetual movement. As settlers, we walk off our frustrations. The medieval Church instituted pilgrimage *on foot* as a cure for homicidal spleen.

Man's real home is not a house, but the Road, and ... life itself is a journey to be walked on foot.

Chronology

1940 13 May: born in Sheffield, 16 June: christened Charles Bruce.

1940-1945 Lives in various places (including Filey on the Yorkshire coast, Birmingham, Stratford, and Derbyshire), moving house at least a dozen times.

1945-1947 On his father's return from the war, the family moves to Birmingham, to a former brothel in Stirling Road.

1947-1961 Lives on a smallholding at Brown's Green, outside Birmingham.

1948-1953 Attends Old School Hall, Wellington, Shropshire.

1953-1958 Attends Marlborough College, Wiltshire.

1954 Plays the role of Mrs Candour in *School for Scandal*.

1958 Engaged as a porter in the Works of Art department at Sotheby's.

1961 Cataloguer in the Impressionist department. Stays with Teddy Millington-Drake at Este, near Venice.
December: first visit to Cairo with Robert Erskine.

1963 August-September: first journey to Afghanistan (and also Istanbul, Cairo, Beirut and Peshawar), with Robert Erskine.

1964 August-September: second journey to Afghanistan, with David Nash.

1965 Problems with eyesight. February–March: travels in Sudan.
21 August: marries Elizabeth Chanler at Geneseo, New York State.
October: Returns to Sotheby's as a director.
December: first journey to Russia.

1966 June: Resigns from Sotheby's.
October: enrols to read archaeology at Edinburgh University.

1967 On an excavation at Zavist, south of Prague. Wins the Wardrop Prize for the 'best first year's work'.

1968 Appointed one of three curators for the exhibition 'The Animal Style' at the Asia House Gallery, New York.
Summer: visits museums in Moscow and Leningrad.
November: leaves Edinburgh without taking his degree.

1969 May: Jonathan Cape commission *The Nomadic Alternative* for an advance of £200.
June–September: third trip to Afghanistan, with Peter Levi.

1970 January: Opening of the Asia House exhibition in New York.
February–March: travels to Dakar, Mauritania, Mali, Morocco; in Mauritania visits the nomadic Nemadi tribe.

1971 29 March–13 April: Teheran, spends five days with the Qashgais on their spring migration.
November: delivers *The Nomadic Alternative*, which is rejected.

1972 January–March: first journey in Dahomey (and Niger and Cameroon). Makes a short film about nomads, now lost.
November: begins job at the *Sunday Times* magazine as arts consultant.

1972–1975 Files ten articles from Paris, Algeria, Peru, Moscow.

1974 December–April 1975: journey to Patagonia.

1976 December: arrives at Cotonou, Benin (formerly Dahomey).

1977 January: coup d'état in Benin; travels to Brazil to research *The Viceroy of Ouidah*.
October: publication of *In Patagonia*.

1978 March: in India, to profile Indira Gandhi.
December: *In Patagonia* is chosen as the book of the year by the *New York Times Book Review*.

1979 January: journey to Haiti.
May: receives the E. M. Forster Award.

1980 Publication of *The Viceroy of Ouidah*.

1982 September: publication of *On the Black Hill*.
November: *On the Black Hill* wins the Whitbread Award for best first novel.
December: trip to Australia.

1983 January–April: travels in Australia, then to Katmandu.
October: appears on BBC television with Borges and Mario Vargas Llosa.

1984 January: South Africa.
March–April: Australia.

1985 December: Hong Kong and Nepal.

1986 January–March: in India, working on *The Songlines*.
August: ill in Switzerland.
September: admitted to Churchill Hospital, Oxford. Diagnosed with AIDS.

1987 January: starts to write *Utz* at Château de Seillans in Provence.
March: in Ghana, where Werner Herzog is filming *The Viceroy of Ouidah*. *The Songlines* is published and becomes a bestseller.

1988 Publication of *Utz*, shortlisted for the Booker Prize.

1989 18 January: dies in Nice.

I The Desert

The best thing is to walk. We should follow the Chinese poet Li Po in 'the hardships of travel and the many branchings of the way'. For life is a journey through a wilderness. This concept, universal to the point of banality, could not have survived unless it were biologically true.

Footprints in the sand

'I know this may sound far-fetched,' I said to Elizabeth Vrba, 'but if I were asked, "What is the big brain for"?, I would be tempted to say, "For singing our way through the wilderness."'

This page and opposite: Dunes

All the Great Teachers have preached that Man, originally, was a 'wanderer in the scorching and barren wilderness of this world' – the words are those of Dostoevsky's Grand Inquisitor – and that to rediscover his humanity, he must slough off attachments and take to the road.

My two most recent notebooks were crammed with jottings taken in South Africa, where I had examined, at first hand, certain evidence on the origin of our species. What I learned there – together with what I now knew about the Songlines – seemed to confirm the conjecture I had toyed with for so long: that Natural Selection has designed us – from the structure of our brain-cells to the structure of our big toe – for a career of seasonal journeys *on foot* through a blistering land of thorn-scrub or desert.

If this were so; if the desert were 'home'; if our instincts were forged in the desert; to survive the rigours of the desert – then it is easier to understand why greener pastures pall on us; why possessions exhaust us, and why Pascal's imaginary man found his comfortable lodgings a prison.

Nazca line, Peru

The surface of the desert is furrowed with a web of straight lines, linking huge geometric forms – triangles, rectangles, spirals, meanders, whip-like zig-zags and superimposed trapezes – that look like the work of a very sensitive and very expensive abstract artist. There are lines as thin as a goat path, and as wide as airport runways. Some converge at a single point, others run on, five miles and more, straddling valleys, and escarpments in their unswerving course. These surface drawings make little sense on the ground, and no aerial photographs do them justice. But from light aircraft you can only gasp with amazement at their scale and the imagination of their makers.

The Pacific Highway cutting across the Nazca lines

The Peruvian desert

28

Grazing horses, Patagonia

Oil wells, Iran

30

Rocky slope

II Passing

Turkish cushions

Shop, Morocco

'Not, of course, that I haven't a few pet theories of my own. I suppose that's why I'm here.'

  'I was wondering that.'

  'What?'

  'What you were doing here.'

'I ask myself, my dear. Every time I brush my teeth I ask the same question. But what would I do in London? Prissy little dinners? Pretty little flat? No. No. Wouldn't suit me at all.'

Ouidah, Dahomey (now Benin)

34

Shop, North-West Africa

This page and opposite: Fish shop, Istanbul

36

Travel must he adventurous. *'The great affair is to move,'* wrote Robert Louis Stevenson in *Travels with a Donkey*, 'to feel the needs and hitches of life more nearly; to come down off this feather bed of civilisation, and find the globe granite underfoot, and strewn with cutting flints.' The bumps are vital. They keep the adrenalin pumping round.

Lisbon: television set recycled as a birdcage

Katmandu, Nepal

Above and overleaf: Fish shop, Istanbul

Butcher's shop, Herat, Afghanistan

Sacred paintings, Kabul, Afghanistan

43

Temple in the Maghreb

44

Painted courtyard, Tunisia

Temple, Khumbu, Nepal

Above and right: Sherpa house, Khumbu

Khumbu, Nepal

48

In France, these notebooks are known as *carnets moleskines:* 'moleskine', in this case, being its black oilcloth binding. Each time I went to Paris, I would buy a fresh supply from a *papeterie* in the Rue de l'Ancienne Comédie. The pages were squared and the end-papers held in place with an elastic band. I had numbered them in series. I wrote my name and address on the front page, offering a reward to the finder. To lose a passport was the least of one's worries: to lose a notebook was a catastrophe.

Untitled

Swat, Pakistan

Catching the bus, Afghanistan

51

Red truck, Pakistan

Painting on a truck, Afghanistan

Painting on a truck, Pakistan

54

Truck, Afghanistan

Truck, Afghanistan

56

Side of a canoe

Untitled

Facade

Roadside shrine, Far East

Soviet poster

Moscow

Soviet Union

Hermitage, Khumbu, Nepal

Sherpa house, Khumbu, Nepal

United States

This page and opposite: Derelict mine, Wyoming

Temple in Bali

Untitled

III 'The Africa I have loved'

Figure on a wall, West Africa

At the edge of the desert, West Africa

70

Figure in tree at sunset, West Africa

This page and opposite: In Mauritania

Not this Africa of blood and slaughter. The Africa I loved was the long undulating savannah country to the north, the 'leopard-spotted land', where flat-topped acacias stretched as far as the eye could see, and there were black-and-white hornbills and tall red termitaries. For whenever I went back to that Africa, and saw a camel caravan, a view of white tents, or a single blue turban far off in the heat haze, I knew that, no matter what the Persians said, Paradise never was a garden but a waste of white thorns.

This page and opposite: Old Nouakchott, Mauritania

74

This page and opposite: West Africa

To the passing visitor there are only two questions. 'Where is my next drink coming from?' and 'Why am I here at all?' And yet, as I write, I remember the desert wind whipping up the green waters; the thin hard blue of the sky; enormous women rolling round the town in pale indigo cotton *boubous*; the shutters on the houses the same hard blue against mud-grey walls; orange bower-birds that weave their basket nests in feathery acacias; gleaming black gardeners sluicing water from leather skins, lovingly, on rows of blue-green onions; lean aristocratic Touaregs, of supernatural appearance, with coloured leather shields and shining spears, their faces encased in indigo veils, which, like carbon paper, dye their skin a thunder-cloud blue; wild Moors with corkscrew curls; firm-breasted Bela girls of the old slave caste, stripped to the waist, pounding at their mortars and keeping time with monotonous tunes; and monumental Songhai ladies with great basket-shaped earrings like those worn by the Queen of Ur over four thousand years ago.

Douala, Cameroon

And at night the half-calabash moon reflected in the river of oxidised silver, rippled with the activity of insects; white egrets roosting in the acacias; the thumping of a *tam-tam* in town; the sound of spontaneous laughter welling up like clear water; the bull frogs, whining mosquitoes that prevented sleep, and on the desert side the far-off howls of jackals or the guard-dogs of nomad camps. Perhaps the Timbuctoo of the mind is more potent than one suspects.

Dakar, Senegal

79

Wall of a house, Mauritania

Above and overleaf: Pisé house, Mali (made of pounded mud and covered with cow dung)

Ruin in the desert

84

We went out into the street. It was grey with the sky overcast. There were shabby concrete buildings, some limp-leaved trees coated with dust, tangles of electric wires and kite-hawks hovering over the refuse dumps. There were ash-grey puddles, iridescent at the edges, and pot-bellied children with green mucus round their noses. There were men going in and out of bars, and old women shuffling round shacks that had been bashed out of oil-drums. Near the railway station, the Chinese found the pharmacy of Dr Shere Malhalua Meji.

The Mosque of Sankové, Timbuktu, Mali

Velvet from raffia, Congo

86

Touareg at an oasis

In Mali

Two men, West Africa

Black township near Johannesburg

Dwellings, West Africa

Abomey, Dahomey (now Benin)

Old priest,
West Africa

West Africa

94

Group of women, West Africa

Camel driver, Sudan

Group of women, West Africa

IV In the footsteps of Robert Byron

Afghanistan

The shrine of ar-Rayy, Iran

Afghanistan (?)

Were he alive today, I think he would agree that, in time (everything in Afghanistan takes time), the Afghans will do something quite dreadful to their invaders – perhaps awaken the sleeping giants of Central Asia.

But that day will not bring back the things we loved: the high, clear days and the blue icecaps on the mountains; the lines of white poplars fluttering in the wind, and the long white prayer-flags; the fields of asphodels that followed the tulips; or the fat-tailed sheep brindling the hills above Chakcharan, and the ram with a tail so big they had to strap it to a cart. We shall not lie on our backs at the Red Castle and watch the vultures wheeling over the valley where they killed the grandson of Genghiz. We will not read Babur's memoirs in his garden at Istalif and see the blind man smelling his way around the rose bushes. Or sit in the Peace of Islam with the beggars of Gazar Gagh. We will not stand on the Buddha's head at Bamiyan, upright in his niche like a whale in a dry-dock. We will not sleep in the nomad tent, or scale the Minaret of Jam. And we shall lose the tastes – the hot, coarse, bitter bread; the green tea flavoured with cardamoms; the grapes we cooled in the snow-melt; and the nuts and dried mulberries we munched for altitude sickness. Nor shall we get back the smell of the beanfields, the sweet, resinous smell of deodar wood burning, or the whiff of a snow leopard at 14,000 feet.

The shrine of Ulgiaitu, Iran

Mosque, Isfahan, Iran

The shrine of Gohar Shad, Herat, Afghanistan

In 1962 – six years before the Hippies wrecked it (by driving educated Afghans into the arms of the Marxists) – you could set off to Afghanistan with the anticipations of, say, Delacroix off to Algiers. On the streets of Herat you saw men in mountainous turbans, strolling hand in hand, with roses in their mouths and rifles wrapped in flowered chintz. In Badakhshan you could picnic on Chinese carpets and listen to the bulbul. In Balkh, the Mother of Cities, I asked a fakir the way to the shrine of Hadji Piardeh. 'I don't know it,' he said. 'It must have been destroyed by Genghiz.'

Mosque, Isfahan, Iran

104

We ended the conversation on Afghanistan, with its pale green rivers and Buddhist monasteries, where eagles wheel over the deodar forests and tribesmen carry copper battle-axes and wreathe vine leaves round their heads as they did in the time of Alexander.

The Minaret of Jam, northern Afghanistan

Mausoleum, Turkey

The shrine of Mahmud, Ghazni, Afghanistan

Minaret, Turkey

We were walking to Persepolis in the rain. The Quashgais were soaked and happy, and the animals were soaked; and when the rain let up, they shook the water from their coats and moved on, as though they were dancing. We passed an orchard with a mud wall around it. There was smell of orange blossom, after rain.

A boy was walking beside me. He and a girl exchanged a flashing glance. She was riding behind her mother on a camel, but the camel was moving faster.

About three miles short of Persepolis we came to some huge domed tents under construction, to which the Shah-i-Shah had invited a riff-raff of royalty for his coronation in June. The tents were designed by the Paris firm of decorators, Jansen.

Someone was yelling, in French.

I tried to get the Quashgai boy to comment, or even to look at the tents. But he shrugged and looked the other way – and so we went on to Persepolis.

Afghanistan

Passing Persepolis I looked at the fluted columns, the porticoes, lions, bulls, griffins; the sleek metallic finish of the stone, and the line on line of megalomaniac inscription: 'I . . . I . . . I . . . The King . . . The King . . . burned . . . slew . . . settled . . .'

My sympathies were with Alexander for burning it.

Again I tried to get the Quashgai boy to look. Again he shrugged. Persepolis might have been made of matchsticks for all he knew or cared – and so we went up to the mountains.

The shrine of Ulgiaitu, Iran

V 'I never liked Jules Verne...'

Windmill, East Anglia, England

Gears

112

Windmill, East Anglia,
England

Prayer flags, Java

Bodnath Stupa, Katmandu, Nepal

Windmill, East Anglia, England

116

Untitled

I never liked Jules Verne, believing that the real was always more fantastic than the fantastical.

Bat cave, Java

Untitled

Altars in the bat cave,
Java

*Prayer flags, Everest
National Park, Nepal*

Euphorbia, Java

Ceremonial poles, Java

123

Untitled

Yaghan tent poles,
Tierra del Fuego

Doll

Angel appearing to the shepherds: 19th-century fresco

Derelict Russian Orthodox church

Wall made of Mani stones, Khumbu, Nepal

128

Prayer flags, Khumbu

Canoes with outriggers, Java

Prayer flags, Khumbu,
Nepal

Temple, Java

Untitled

Tomb at Kafiristan, Afghanistan

133

Ferris wheel, Sind, Pakistan

134

Windmill, East Anglia, England

VI In Patagonia

This page and opposite: Welsh family, Gaimán

One afternoon in the early 70s, in Paris, I went to see the architect and designer Eileen Gray, who at the age of ninety-three thought nothing of a fourteen-hour working day. She lived in the rue Bonaparte, and in her salon hung a map of Patagonia, which she had painted in gouache.

'I've always wanted to go there,' I said. 'So have I,' she added. 'Go there for me.' I went. I cabled the *Sunday Times:* 'Have Gone to Patagonia'. In my rucksack I took Mandelstam's *Journey to Armenia* and Hemingway's *In Our Time*. Six months later I came back with the bones of a book that, this time, did get published. While stringing its sentences together, I thought that telling stories was the only conceivable occupation for a superfluous person such as myself. I am older and a bit stiffer, and I am thinking of settling down. Eileen Gray's map now hangs in my apartment. But the future is tentative.

Welsh farmhouse

Welsh farmhouse, interior

English estancia, Tierra del Fuego

English ranch, interior

Corral for cattle

Reflections in a window

Left: Tins in a niche in a rock

There was no sound but the wind, whirring through thorns and whistling through dead grass, and no other sign of life but a hawk, and a black beetle easing over white stones.

The Patagonian desert is not a desert of sand or gravel, but a low thicket of grey-leaved thorns which give off a bitter smell when crushed. Unlike the deserts of Arabia it has not produced any dramatic excess of the spirit, but it does have a place in the record of human experience. Charles Darwin found its negative qualities irresistible. In summing up *The Voyage of the Beagle*, he tried, unsuccessfully, to explain why, more than any of the wonders he had seen, these 'arid wastes' had taken such firm possession of his mind.

In the 1860s W.H.Hudson came to the Río Negro looking for the migrant birds that wintered around his home in La Plata. Years later he remembered the trip through the filter of his Notting Hill boarding-house and wrote a book so quiet and sane it makes Thoreau seem a ranter. Hudson devotes a whole chapter of *Idle Days in Patagonia* to answering Mr Darwin's question, and he concludes that desert wanderers discover in themselves a primeval calmness (known also to the simplest savage), which is perhaps the same as the Peace of God.

141

Peasant with his granddaughter

Welsh farmer, Gaimán

The grave of Wilson and Evans

143

Old Dodge

Transport in Patagonia

Cemetery, Santa Cruz

Cemetery

Giant statue dedicated to the oil-well drillers

 *The opera singer*

 *Landscape*

147

Charlie Milward's house

A house in Punta Arenas

View from a cave

148

Prehistoric cave paintings, Río de las Pinturas

Charlie Milward's foundry at Punta Arenas

A wreck on the beach at Punta Arenas

Tomb, Punta Arenas

Landscape

Landscape with dog

151

Left and above: The Moreno glacier at Lake Argentina

The cave at Last Hope Sound

Jaramillo station

Inhabitant of the island of Chiloé

Butch Cassidy's log cabin in Cholila

In Patagonia

VII Meetings

In Java

Peruvian Train

Men in shadow, Afghanistan

*Elizabeth Chatwin in
a bus, Afghanistan*

Tree

Poppies, England

Untitled

Previous page and right:
Maria Reiche

Yak, Everest National Park, Nepal

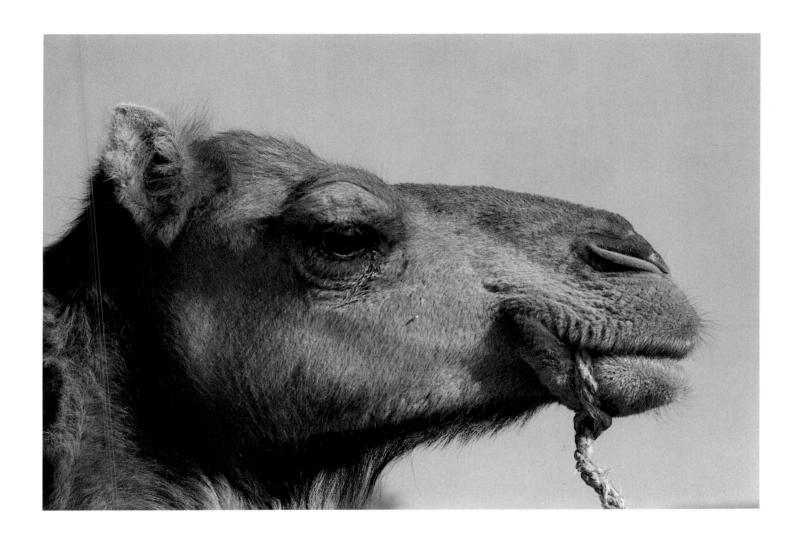

Camel

Sheep dyed with henna, Afghanistan

Kardamili, Mani, Greece

Boy with chicken, West Africa

Left and opposite: Men

White poplars in spring

Lake, Afghanistan

Lizard

Euphorbia

Bird in cage, Afghanistan

Sea cadet, Turkey

Graffiti

Everest National Park, Nepal

The photographs in this section were provided by the
Royal Museum of Central Africa, Tervuren, Belgium

IX A sense for surfaces

African flags

. . . photographs by someone with an unerring sense of composition.

Bruce Chatwin on Wilfred Thesiger.

The Peruvian desert

Lichen, Afghanistan

Wall of a stupa, Surat, Pakistan

Northern Afghanistan

180

Russian icon, detail

Chairs

181

At the shrine of Ansari, Gazar Gah, Herat, Afghanistan

182

Painted shopfront, Nouakchott

Painted pirogue, Mauritania

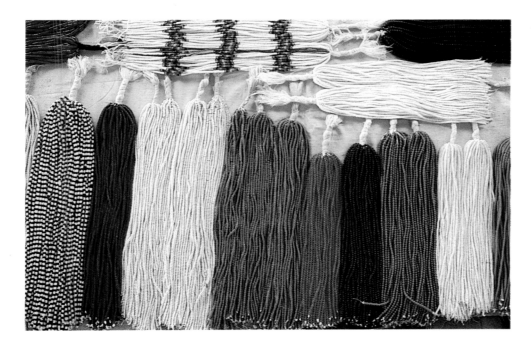

Glass beads, Katmandu

Flower garlands, India

185

The Moors have a passion for the colour blue. Their robes are blue. Their turbans are blue. The tents of the *bidonville* are patched with blue cotton; and the shanties, cobbled together from packing cases, are bound to have some blue paint somewhere.

This afternoon I followed a wizened old crone who was picking over the garbage dump in search of blue rag. She picked up one piece. She picked up another. She compared them. She chucked the first piece away. At last she found a scrap which was exactly the shade she was looking for – and she went away singing.

Windmill, East Anglia, England

186

Construction work, Dakar, Senegal

He alone in the west understood the quality in art the Japanese call 'wabi'. Literally the word means 'poverty', but applied to a work of art it means that true beauty, 'the beauty that breaks away from this world', must rely on the use of its humblest materials.

Wood

Chadors, Afghanistan

Sources

p.   19   *Anatomy of Restlessness*, Jonathan Cape, London, 1996, p. 3.

p.   19   Ibid., p. 101.

p.   20   *The Songlines*, Jonathan Cape, London, 1987, p. 5.

p.   20   *Anatomy of Restlessness*, p. 8.

p.   21   *What Am I Doing Here*, Jonathan Cape, London, 1989, p. 222.

p.   21   Ibid., p. 273.

p.   23   *Anatomy of Restlessness*, p. 103.

p.   24   *The Songlines*, p. 249

p.   25   Ibid., p. 161.

p.   26   *What Am I Doing Here*, p. 94.

p.   33   *The Songlines*, p. 46.

p.   37   *Anatomy of Restlessness*, p. 102.

p.   49   *The Songlines*, p. 160

p.   73   *What Am I Doing Here*, p. 25.

pp.   78-9 *Anatomy of Restlessness*, p. 28.

p.   85   *What Am I Doing Here*, p. 47.

pp.   100-1   Ibid., p. 293.

p.   103   Ibid., p. 287.

p.   105   Ibid., p. 135.

pp.   108-9 *The Songlines*, pp. 185-6

p.   118   *Anatomy of Restlessness*, p. 9.

p.   136   Ibid., pp. 13-14.

p.   141   *In Patagonia*, Jonathan Cape, London, 1977, p. 15.

p.   161   *What Am I Doing Here*, p. 94.

p.   178   *Anatomy of Restlessness*, p. 109.

p.   186   *The Songlines*, p. 171.

p.   188   *Anatomy of Restlessness*, p. 67.